Mastering the Piano

CD enclosed

Level 3

A 7-Volume Series of Motivating Performance Repertoire

Carole L. Bigler &
Valery Lloyd-Watts

Alfred

Foreword

People who play the piano, whether casually, seriously, or professionally, favor learning pieces they enjoy and avoid practicing those that don't appeal to them. Teachers know that the more students love the repertoire, the more motivated they will be to learn it. Consequently, a motivated pianist is a successful pianist. The repertoire in this seven-volume series has been chosen specifically for its appeal both to performers and audiences, and is intended as a resource for selecting performance material.

Features of this series:

- Pieces are accessible to students. Many have repeated or parallel passages, decreasing the learning time and creating a feeling of accomplishment.

- Repertoire contains music of the great masters from all eras, and provides exposure to the full range of human emotion.

- Pieces are in approximate order of difficulty; however, it is not necessary to follow the printed order or to learn every piece.

- A CD, performed by Valery Lloyd-Watts, accompanies this book as a guide for appropriate musical interpretation. The dynamic and metronome markings in the score correspond with the recorded performances. The metronome markings are meant to be guides rather than strict boundaries.

The music in this book is the product of our love for expressive and exciting piano music and our experience in working with thousands of pianists of all ages and abilities.

Contents

Grand Waltz

Muzio Clementi
(1752–1832)

Track 1　**Allegro** (♩. = 63)

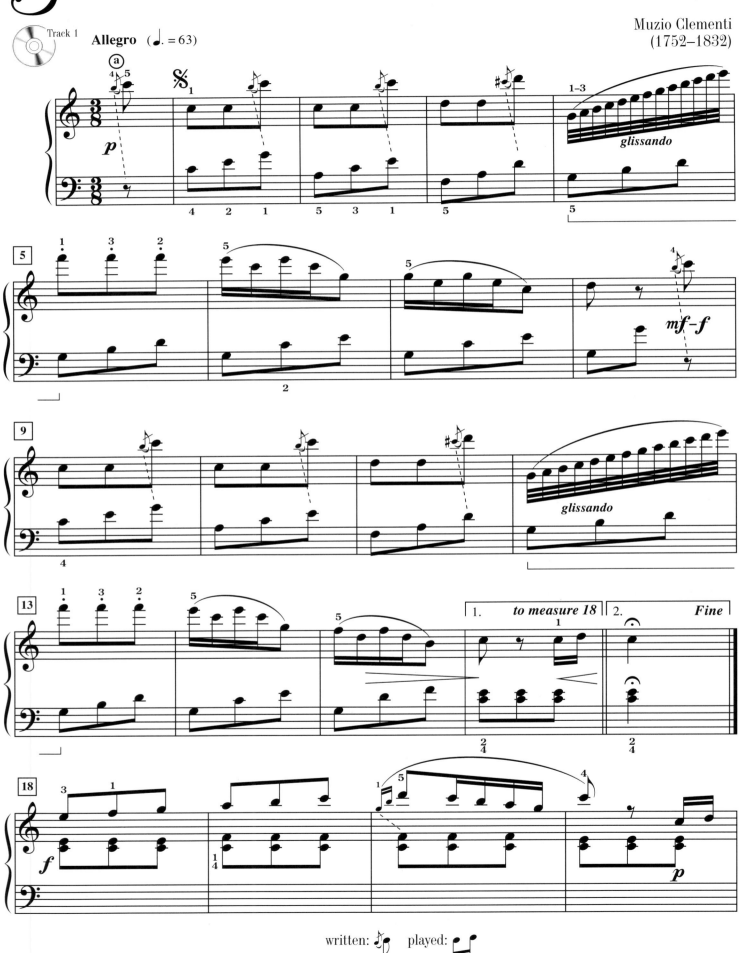

written: 　　played:

ⓐ All appoggiaturas are played on the beat.

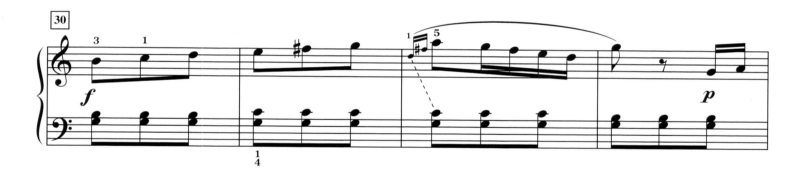

Sonata in C Major

Track 2

Domenico Scarlatti (1685–1757)
K. 95; L. 358

Allegro (♩. = 112)

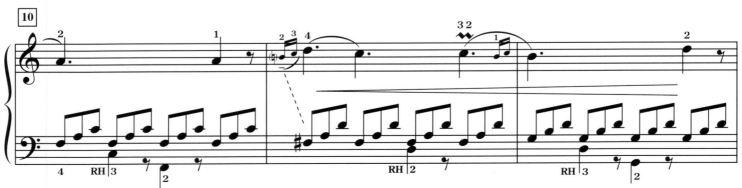

(a) Arpeggiate the chord the first time. Play the trill on the repeat only.

Étude in G Minor

Track 3

Cornelius Gurlitt (1820–1901)
Op. 82, No. 99

Sonatina in C Major (Third Movement)

Track 4

Muzio Clementi (1752–1832)
Op. 36, No. 3

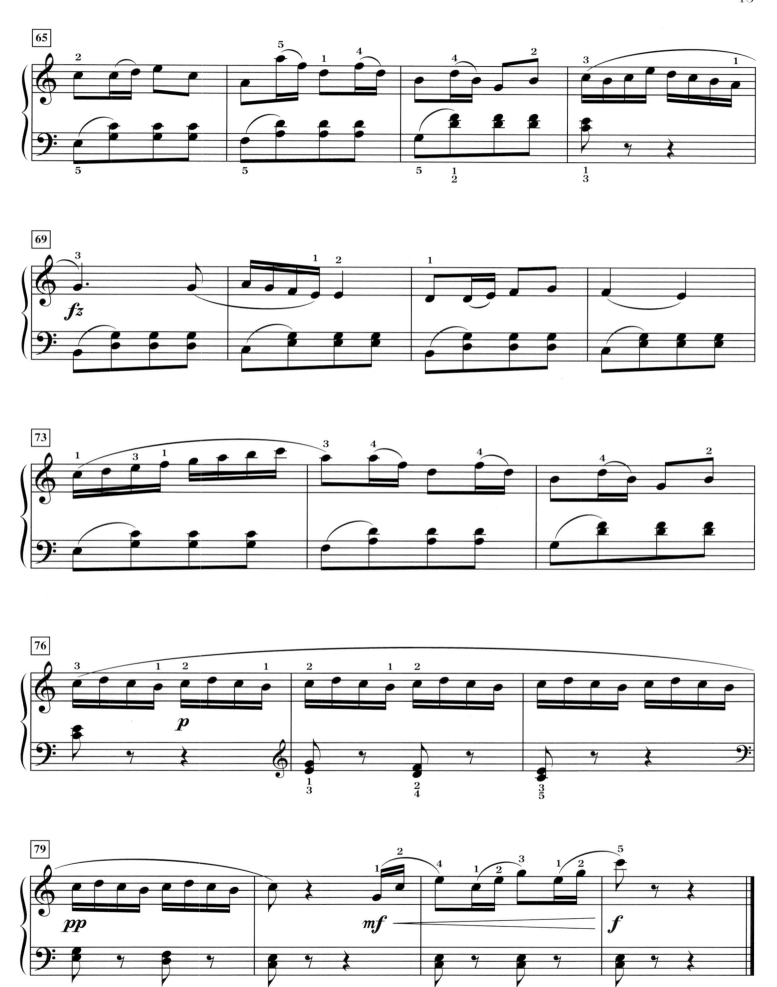

L'Orage (The Storm)

Friedrich Burgmüller (1806–1874)
Op. 109, No. 13

Track 5

Solfegietto

Track 6

Carl Philipp Emanuel Bach
(1714–1788)

(a) Small notes are optional.

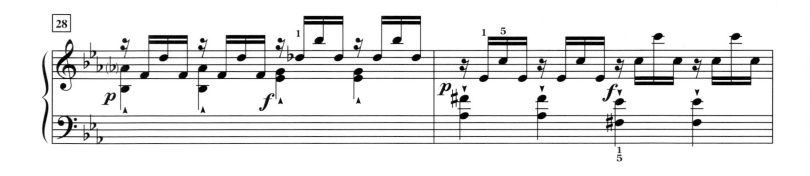

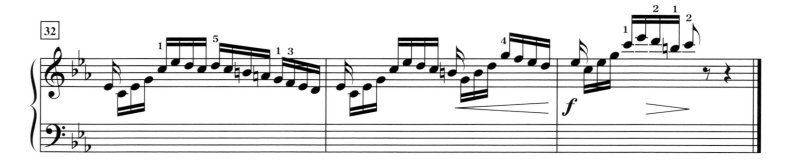

Waltz in A Minor

Track 7

Frédéric Chopin (1810–1849)
Posthumous

The Pearls

Friedrich Burgmüller (1806–1874)
Op. 109, No. 2

Track 8

ⓐ Play the small notes softly to distinguish them from the melody notes.

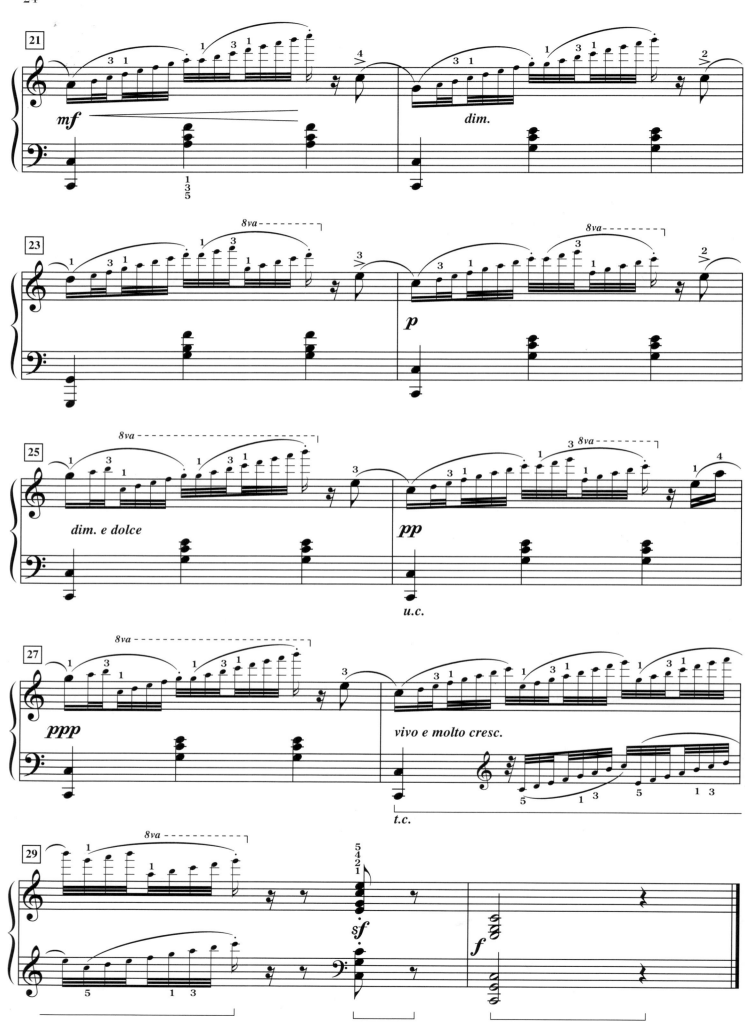